BUSY DAY, B[USY NIGHT]

Rain Forest

📖 **SCHOLASTIC**

Children's Press®
A Division of Scholastic Inc.
New York Toronto London Auckland Sydney Mexico City
New Delhi Hong Kong Danbury, Connecticut

Early Childhood
Consultants:

Ellen Booth Church
Diane Ohanesian

3 4 5 6 7 8 9 10 R 19 18 17 16 15 14 13 12 11 10   62

Library of Congress Cataloging-in-Publication Data

Hendra, Sue.
  Busy day, busy night : rain forest / Sue Hendra.
    p. cm.
    ISBN-13: 978-0-531-24407-4 (lib. bdg.)   ISBN-13: 978-0-531-24582-8 (pbk.)
    ISBN-10: 0-531-24407-5 (lib. bdg.)   ISBN-10: 0-531-24582-9 (pbk.)
  1. Rain forests–Juvenile literature. I. Title.

  QH86.H46 2010
  578.734–dc22   2009005499

The sun is shining.

But rain falls down,

down,

down.

It is a busy day.
Where?
The rain forest!

Who is busy?
Let's see.

Wild pigs
GRUNT.

Turtles
CRAWL.

Frogs
**hop,
hop,
hop!**

7

Spider monkeys **LEAP.**

Ants **MARCH,**

MARCH, MARCH!

9

Howler monkeys SWiNG.

A sloth HANGS UPSIDE DOWN.

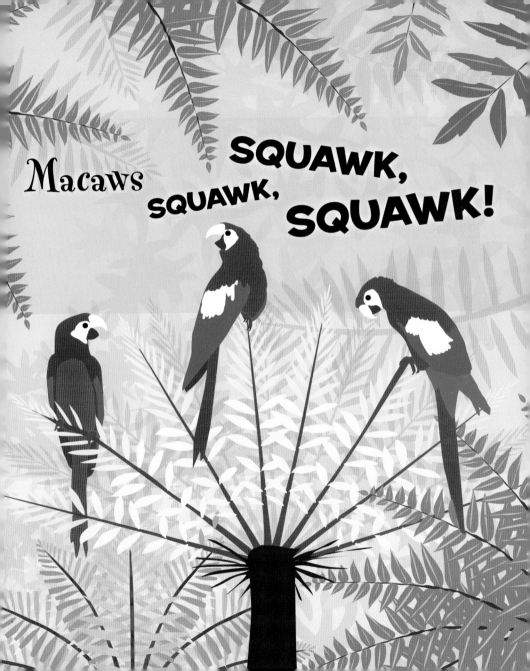

An eagle feeds her baby.

Blue
butterflies FLY,

FLY,

FLY, FLY!

Everyone is busy.

The sun sets.

The moon rises.

Some animals go to sleep.

Some animals wake up.

15

It is a busy night. Where?

The rain forest!

Who is busy?
Let's see.

A jaguar **hunts.**

16

A tapir
swims, swims, swims!

17

A boa slithers.

Fruit bats **flap, flap, flap!**

19

Tree frogs **BLINK.**

Owl monkeys

squeak,

squeak, squeak!

Everyone is busy.

The moon sets.

The sun rises.

Some animals go to sleep.

Some animals wake up.

It is another busy day.
Where?
The rain forest!

Rookie Storytime Tips

Busy Day, Busy Night: Rain Forest introduces daytime and nighttime animals that live in the lush habitat of the rain forest. As you and your preschooler read this book together, offer plenty of opportunities for him or her to point to and name the animals. It's a fun way to foster the recognition of rain forest animals— an important part of the preschool curriculum.

Invite your child to go back and find the following. Along the way, he or she will build knowledge of the difference between nocturnal and diurnal animals— another part of the preschool curriculum.

BAT Is this bat awake during the DAY or during the NIGHT?

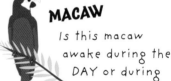

MACAW Is this macaw awake during the DAY or during the NIGHT?

JAGUAR Is this jaguar awake during the DAY or during the NIGHT?

Ask your child if he or she can:
SQUAWK like a macaw? **Blink** like a tree frog?
Flap like a fruit bat?